ST BENEDICT AND CHRISTIANITY IN ENGLAND

SAINT BENEDICT

AND CHRISTIANITY

IN ENGLAND

Patrick Barry OSB

Abbot of Ampleforth

Ampleforth Abbey Press
(Distributed by Gracewing)

AMPLEFORTH ABBEY PRESS
AMPLEFORTH ABBEY
YORK
from
Gracewing
Fowler Wright Books
Southern Avenue, Leominster
Herefordshire HR6 0QF

Printed at the Cromwell Press
Typeset at Ampleforth Abbey
in Monotype Bembo

ISBN 0 85244 338 2

CONTENTS

ST BENEDICT AND CHRISTIANITY IN ENGLAND

Introduction

JANE AUSTEN in her youthful History of England did not have a very high opinion of King Henry VIII. "The crimes and cruelties of this prince," she wrote, "were too numerous to be mentioned....and nothing can be said in his vindication, but that his abolishing Religious Houses and leaving them to the ruinous depredations of time has been of infinite use to the landscape of England in general." Jane Austen's not so gentle irony reflects an attitude that still survives. That Abbeys look best in ruins, with its presumed corollary that monks are best safely dead, is certainly a view one comes across from time to time. Quite recently I met a group outside the Abbey Church at Ampleforth who asked me: "Is this an Abbey?" When I told them it is, one of them said in a sceptical and disappointed voice: "Then where are the ruins?"

This assumption that Abbeys should be ruins is re-enforced by the use of what remains of ancient Abbeys to attract tourists. Yet a visit may make one wonder whether an interest in ruins is a very vibrant sign of interest in life. There are deeper and more important reasons for investigating Benedictine Abbeys and what they stood for and still stand for. The simple truth is that the origins of Christianity in this country were strictly monastic. Both the Roman and the Celtic missions were monastic not only in the origins of those who brought the Christian gospel to the country, but in the very method and manner of communicating the faith.

Then there is another truth, which may to some seem surprising. It is the fact that monks still exist and, however alarming that may seem, they have a significant contribution to make to the future of Christianity in our world of today. It is a world which reflects, in a different way, some of the darkness during which monasticism first emerged in these islands. It is a world in which gospel belief (for which those early monks lived) has been fading away from the realities of the lives we live. Arnold Toynbee wrote fifty years ago: "We have for a number of generations past been living on spiritual capital, I mean clinging to Christian practice without possessing the Christian belief – and practice unsupported by belief is a wasting asset." [1] There is a new desolation about us, not at all unlike that of Saint Augustine of Canterbury's day; in its spiritual dimension it is not so far away from the darkness of the break up of Rome. The secularist world is strong in many respects, but its shadow-side is spiritual emptiness and the absence so many experience today of anything ultimate to live for. It raises the question whether monastic witness is the strong sign of faith and the following of Christ which could help men and women, as it did in the past, to a revival of spiritual life and hope. If so, a good beginning would be to understand the ideals of christian living which are expressed in the Rule of Benedict.

St Benedict and His Times

Saint Benedict seems too remote from modern England to matter very much. He came from Italy and spent all his life there, but he was himself too ancient to be an Italian; they hadn't been invented in his day. He lived mostly in the sixth century – a time of turmoil, uncertainty, the death of many hopes and ideals. It was a time when what everyone had thought of as the impregnable might of Rome was falling to pieces before men's eyes. It took quite a long time. The first sack of Rome was in AD 410 and more that 100 years later barbarian kingdoms were in fashion all over the western Roman world; but they weren't all completely anti-Roman, once they had done a bit of sacking and looting. In fact some of them tried to imitate Roman institutions closely with uneven success. Rome was the one and only model of power and government they knew. They tried to imitate what they had destroyed. In a sense they wanted everything to go on as before but with the addition of a little barbarian panache.

However, the new barbarian kingdom in Italy failed to impress. Justinian was at the time of St Benedict Emperor in Constantinople. He decided that all he had to do was to restore order again with a strong army for the reconquest of Italy. Then Roman power would go on for ever – just as it was always meant to. The attempt under Belisarius his general was ruinous to Italy, devastating for the people and limitless in the human agony it caused – just as in Bosnia today; not only charity and Christian values but common sanity itself seem to be swamped in horror after horror. Most of Italy was like that in the sixth and seventh centuries.

3

That was the world of St Benedict – the world of Europe, as Roman power disintegrated leaving pockets of civilisations' remnants, and pockets of sheer barbarism in the midst of imposing and now useless ruins. And the great Roman roads, which had been built to last, fanned out in all directions to provide a way for the wild war-lords into the heart of the people. It was a time when there was no peace, no security and no vision. It was a time that cried out for inspiration and direction.

St Benedict was born in Norcia. He went to Rome for study, but he turned away from whatever face of that troubled world he met there. He decided to seek God alone and seek sanity in doing so. St Gregory knew something of the world from which Benedict turned as he looked for a way to find more lasting values; and in this connection he described Benedict as "*scienter nescius et sapienter indoctus*" – knowingly unknowing and wisely untaught. He found a lonely mountain 40 miles from Rome at Subiaco. The gorge was wild but at its foot was a deserted memorial of Roman luxury – a pleasure villa of Nero's and an artificial lake. Benedict climbed up the cliff face and lived in a cave to be alone, to pray and to surrender his life utterly to God. The cave is still there and the monastery later built round it out of the air and the cliff-face. Nero's villa was in time swept away when the lake burst its dam. Nothing of it is left today.

Benedict went away from that sad and disintegrating world of Rome in order to seek God alone in the severe life of a hermit. But here comes the first difference in him from many others who before and after sought to preserve their sanity and the 'new life' to which Christ called the baptised. He wanted to be left alone, but others sought his guidance and help; Benedict responded. Instead of the solitary search for God, on which he had embarked to start with, he taught them to seek God together in community. Benedictine monks and nuns are those who follow that way in the strength of common prayer and a common life.

Then, persecution drove him from Subiaco and he founded the great monastery of Monte Cassino. There he wrote his Rule for Monks, which is the only surviving writing he left. His manuscript was treasured at Cassino by his monks. He died in 547. His life had spanned a period of dramatic change from the last uncertain flare-ups of the light of Roman order to the darkness which to most who lived through it seemed terminal. In fact it preceded the dawn of Europe. The last of the invaders – the terrible Lombards – sacked Monte Cassino 34 years after Benedict's death. They left it in ruins – the ruination, as it seemed, of all Benedict's work. It was not, however, the end but a new beginning. The monks themselves escaped and carried the manuscript of the Rule to Rome. The monastery they founded on the Cœlian Hill was the monastery from which St Augustine of Canterbury set out in 597 under orders from the Pope, St Gregory the Great, to convert the wild and heathen inhabitants of England.

Benedict, then, had fled from a disintegrating world. He had been driven by violence from his first attempt at stable community life. The violence of the Gothic war beset his life at Monte Cassino. Soon after his death the monastery was destroyed by the Lombards in 581 and it was not until 136 years later that a new Benedictine monastery was built on the Monte Cassino site. But the Rule itself was safely taken to Rome from where in due course it spread out over the whole of Europe and every other continent after that.

5

Anyone who believes that "there's a divinity that shapes our ends, rough-hew them how we will" [2] may be inclined to see the hand of God in the way the text of the Rule of St Benedict was preserved. To others it may seem to be no more than a matter of historical luck. But there is one strange point to be noted. The Rule was written for Benedict's own community in his own time. You might expect it to be stamped so firmly with the ethos, the assumptions and the limitations of Italy in the sixth century that it could never be transplanted to other times and other climates. You might expect it to be nothing but an historical curiosity; but it is not so. The text assumes that the Abbot should have the liberty to apply the Rule differently in different times and different places. You find in it just that firmness about principle with understanding about application that gave it a life that is still vigorous in other times, other climates and other cultures.

The Rule for Monks

THE RULE OF SAINT BENEDICT is a work of great spiritual vision and human insight. That is why it has lasted as a valid guide to men and women for fourteen hundred years. It is concerned above all with the sincere and faithful following of Christ. "Let them put nothing whatever before the love of Christ" is Benedict's last piece of advice for his monks. The sources from which he draws are principally scriptural. His approach is always moderate, sane, understanding. He wrote the Rule as a guide for monks who were called to live a life apart, a life of special dedication to which they felt called in prayer; but it was a life also in close communion with the local church and its bishop.

He understood how men and women are called to make prayer a central factor in their lives, and he urged his monks to see that call as coming from Christ himself – like his call to the disciples to leave everything and follow him. It was a call which could be refused, as the rich young man refused it, or it could be accepted, as Peter, James and John accepted it. It was this call or 'vocation' with which Benedict was concerned in writing his Rule, and he always has the dimension of personal response to God in mind. The Rule is not primarily a legal document and it is not cast in legal jargon. It has practical directions, but they are far fewer than in other comparable Rules. Benedict even suggests that another Abbot might like to vary some of his provisions – on the assumption, of course, that his overall aim was the same.

When it came to the central question of commitment, this was St Benedict's requirement: a monk takes a vow of

Stability which commits him for life to one community; he takes a vow of Obedience (which should come naturally, he says, to those who "count nothing dearer to themselves than Christ"); he takes a vow of Conversion of life to the monastic way, which includes a common life, common prayer, a life of God-centred celibacy and the absolute renunciation of every form of private property. It was a life in which monks should earn their living and also keep alive the knowledge of Scripture and the Fathers of the Church by regular daily reading and deep reflection on what they read in an ambience of recollection and silence. Thus the monasteries which followed the Rule quite naturally became oases of peace, of the cultivation of the land, of creativity, of learning and of teaching. They were seed-beds of an emerging Christian civilisation throughout Europe.

St Benedict's Rule was not at the time the only Rule for monks. There were many other monastic rules, from some of which St Benedict borrowed, but none of the others achieved the prestige which the Benedictine Rule gradually won throughout western Europe. This success was due to its qualities of wisdom, moderation and spiritual insight. He relied very strongly on the Word of Scripture. He was building also on the foundation of those who had gone before him and he had learnt from them.

The beginnings of monasticism sprang straight from the gospel. That is why any renewal of monastic life through the ages has come always from that same source – the pure teaching of the gospel. It all started in AD 270 with St Antony of Egypt. As a young man he went to church one day and heard the gospel text read out: "If you would be perfect, go, sell all that you have and come follow me." He responded immediately and did just that. He never looked back and went out into the desert to a solitary life of prayer. Prayer was the centre then, as it was ever afterwards, for those who seek God as monks. In the subsequent century thousands followed his example all over the Middle East living solitary lives as hermits or a life of Christian brotherhood or sisterhood in closely regulated communities. The idea spread rapidly to the West under the influence of John Cassian and others.

There are many examples of Benedict's humanity in the Rule, particularly in his instructions to the Abbot; for instance Benedict says: "that he should seek to be loved rather than feared;" "that he should give the strong something to strive for without frightening the weak;" "that he should have special care of the old and young;" "that he should never act without taking advice." Then, in a wine-drinking country, he is gentle in his comment: "We read that monks should never have wine, but nowadays they cannot be persuaded of this, so let us at least agree on this – that they should not go on drinking until they are full."

St Benedict had started in Subiaco in a life of prayer and penance as a hermit. When he set up his communities they also led a life separate from the laity. Yet from the very first the monasteries were an inspiration to laity as well as to the monks and nuns who gave their lives to God according to the Rule. The tradition of Benedictine hospitality takes its origin from the Rule, in which St Benedict tells his monks that guests "are to be welcomed as Christ." Through hospitality as well as through example the monasteries became centres of spiritual inspiration. Their influence grew in other ways. They became centres of learning and education and centres of employment. The inspiration of the Rule's spiritual vision thus in many ways went beyond the monastery walls and that has continued to happen in a quite exceptional way in our day since Vatican II. All over the world men and women in lay life, who desire to seek God more faithfully, have found in the Rule just that inspiration and guidance they need. There is something timeless in what St Benedict wrote. He addresses those deep and constant and changeless spiritual themes which are essentially the same for all. In a time of uncertainty and doubt many feel that the vision of the Rule has applications in lay life also.

In Benedict's lifetime the Rule probably did not penetrate beyond Monte Cassino and a few other monasteries. It was the destruction of the monastery that brought it to a wider public. When the monks of Monte Cassino in the sixth century escaped from the savage Lombards who destroyed their monastery they took with them to Rome a treasure of inestimable value – the actual copy of the Rule which had been written by St Benedict himself. That was the providential beginning of Benedictine growth and influence. But the manner in which that influence grew was complex and slow.

Gregory and Augustine

SAINT GREGORY was a very great man. He had been Prefect of Rome and showed his idea of how to put the Roman world on the right lines by founding seven monasteries. It was his way of spreading the gospel and civilisation. Then he gave his money away and joined his own monastery on the Cœlian Hill just to show how much he meant it. He wanted nothing so much as to be a simple monk, devoted to God, to prayer, to reading, to peace, but like many after him he was taken from his monastery and sent into the world of affairs on a diplomatic mission to Constantinople. Then the Romans made him Pope. He pacified the Lombards and established firm government in Italy to check all the devastation of that terrible century. He was familiar with east and west. He organised the church throughout western Europe with a coherent plan for the dioceses he created. He wrote on pastoral practice, on how to deal with existing pagan practices and prejudices in an understanding and temperate way. He must have had a unique overview of the chaos of Europe and the threats from all sides. He certainly had a firm and positive vision of how to rebuild the church and society. At a terrible time he became the one centre of sound guidance and authority in the West.

Then suddenly he did something which must have appeared to his contemporaries completely mad and irrelevant to the real problems of the time. Whether or not there is anything in that old story about the English slave boys, whom he thought looked more like angels than Angles when he saw them in Rome, Gregory certainly showed love for the pagan

11

English – that particular sort of love which comes from the purest sources of Christianity. He looked over a Europe from which hope had drained and faith was in its death throes. He fixed his eyes on England and sent Augustine with forty monks to convert it.

Why ever did he send monks, who had withdrawn from the world, for a work like that? He knew about St Benedict, who had died only fifty years before and wrote about him. He knew that monks, like Benedict, turned away from the world and its values; yet he sent Augustine to an active and perilous life in England. He didn't do any of the elaborate planning that would be called for in our day. Something drove him to act dramatically by sending the monks on the urgent task of evangelisation without preparation for them, except the wise and solid personal guidance he gave them.

Augustine and his monks had not gone far on the way to England when, as they heard and thought about the appalling outpost to which Gregory was sending them, they were, according to Bede, "paralysed with terror. They began to contemplate returning home rather than going to a barbarous, fierce, and unbelieving nation whose language they did not even understand."

Gregory was unimpressed when Augustine referred back to Rome to propose the abandonment of so outlandish an enterprise. He instructed Augustine to persevere, made him a bishop to encourage him and told him how to handle the wild men of Kent. "It would have been better," wrote Gregory, "never to have begun so good a work rather than let your foreboding turn you back. You must, my dear sons, show the greatest zeal in pressing ahead to complete the good work you have begun. You mustn't let the trials of the journey, nor the malicious tongues of reporters put you off."

Things worked out very much better than Augustine could have expected. Martyrdom was not for him. In less than a year the King of Kent was converted and brought his people with him. The monks' method is described by Bede: "They began to imitate the way of life of the apostles and of the primitive church. They were constantly engaged in prayers, in vigils and fasts; they preached the word of life to as many as they could. They despised all worldly things as foreign to them; they accepted only the necessaries of life from those whom they taught; in all things they practiced what they preached and kept themselves prepared to endure adversities, even to the point of dying for the truths they proclaimed." [3]

This successful example of monastic evangelisation, like monasticism itself, was closely based on the New Testament. The peaceful conversion of southern England was a triumph for the quiet witness of missionary monasticism which focussed on the power of prayer and on the witness of community life. Gregory wrote to congratulate Augustine, to attribute his success to God's grace, and to warn him against pride in his achievement.

Gregory's sense of the power of prayer and the unity of Christians in the communion of saints is shown in another letter in which he tells Eulogius, Patriarch of Alexandria, of Augustine's success in baptising the English who lived in a far off corner of the world (*in mundi angulo*) and he expresses his belief that Eulogius' prayer was an important reason for Augustine's success. In those wild days there was much to confuse and frighten them, but they did have clear perspectives and priorities. They did believe really in prayer and in the communion of saints, and in the power of that prayer-centred communion. Gregory saw the whole church from Egypt to England as one – especially as one in prayer.

Augustine and his followers were monks and their whole approach to the conversion of England was monastic, but were they Benedictines? There is (in the fastidious language of historians) no evidence that the monastic rule St Augustine brought with him was the Rule of St Benedict. But equally there is no evidence that it was not. It is not certain but it is highly probable that Augustine had St Benedict's Rule with him when he landed in Kent. It was not long before the Rule of St Benedict was established in England as the norm for monks. There is a manuscript of the Rule in the Bodleian which was written at Canterbury in about 700. It is the oldest English Manuscript of the Rule. It is written in a large uncial hand with large margins and fine but restrained initial letters. There can be no doubt about the status of St Benedict's Rule by that time – some 100 years after St Augustine's arrival. It is attractive to think that the moderation and sanity of St Benedict influenced those early monks in their smooth and successful evangelisation of the emerging English nation. Later in the eighth century Charlemagne turned to England and summoned Alcuin of York to provide the essential inspiration of the Carolingian Renaissance. The monasteries were crucial to Charlemagne's plan and they were unquestionably Benedictine. In fact it is said that Charlemagne asked: "Are there any other Rules except St Benedict's?" The Rule was firmly established throughout Europe.

Celtic Monasticism in Britain

SAINT AUGUSTINE'S mission was to the new invaders from overseas. There had been a strong Christian church in Roman Britain but it had been destroyed with the rest of that society. Augustine came from Rome to reconvert the country, starting in the south. It may seem strange to those unfamiliar with the history of the time that just before he arrived in Kent there was another mission to convert the country starting in Scotland and moving to Northumbria. It came from the strong celtic church in Ireland and it also was monastic. It is even stranger to reflect that the origins of that celtic monasticism are to be found among the Christians of Roman Britain a century earlier.

I follow the magisterial work of Bishop Anthony Hanson in seeing St Patrick as a Romano-Briton of the early fifth century, who not only evangelised the Irish but gave them their strong monastic orientation. Patrick, when he escaped from slavery in Ireland, may, as Hanson thinks, have been influenced by monastic circles in Britain; but Gaulish monasticism is more likely to have been his real inspiration. Certainly the Church he left in Ireland was so monastic that the influence of Abbots towered above that of Bishops. It was a strange arrangement, which has sometimes seemed attractive to Abbots; it did not outlive the arrival of the Normans. The monks themselves in their mode of life were influenced, in spite of the climate, by the more extreme exemplars of asceticism from the deserts of Egypt and Syria. Today you can still get an idea of the extremity of their penitential life from the monastic remains on the island of

Skellig off the western coast of Ireland. Their zeal for extremes was in contrast to Benedictine moderation, but they also were missionaries. There was a curious twist to their missionary zeal. The Irish were home-loving, nostalgic, and they were (at least in the sixth century) reasonably secure in their remote island. They were thus deprived of persecution and the prospect of martyrdom. The ultimate sacrifice of self for Christ was to go abroad to convert the pagans who knew not Christ – wherever they could be found. They thought the end of the world was near. They knew Christ had said that the gospel must first be preached to the whole world. They were anxious to hasten things on by dealing themselves with any who had not heard it. There is a story in one of the Chronicles of two Irish monks landing on the coast of Sussex in a coracle. They were disappointed on learning that the inhabitants were already Christian. They got into their coracle again and sailed off into the unknown in search of more promising material for conversion.

These celtic monks evangelised Scotland in the mid-sixth century. "Columba," says Bede, "turned (the Picts) to the faith of Christ by his words and example and so received the island of Iona from them in order to establish a monastery there." Aidan and Cuthbert followed him with many others in bringing the faith to Northumbria and Lindisfarne. Their memory remains more tenaciously in the North than that of Augustine and his monks in the South. But both were monastic in their way of life and their way of preaching. The great flowering of Christianity in the seventh and eighth centuries, before the next devastation of the destroyers from Scandinavia, was the fruit of monasticism. It inspired the conversion of Germany by the English monk Boniface.

Boniface (680 – 754) is worthy of special note. He was an English monk, born in Crediton of Saxon parents, who conceived a longing to convert his own people in Germany. He was true heir to the Gregory/Augustine tradition of the missionary monk; this is illustrated by his zeal to learn more about Gregory's letters to Augustine and his interest in Augustine's methods at Canterbury. Like Gregory he saw prayer as the mainspring of missionary activity and the source of unity. He worked closely with the Frankish court and inspired the reform of the Frankish Church before going on to convert Germany and establish the Rule of St Benedict there. He did much to establish and strengthen the influence of the Pope in the Frankish and German churches before being martyred by the pagans in Frisia. He was an English European (perhaps the greatest of them all) before ever Europe had become a political concept.

Anglo-Saxon Christianity inspired also the conversion of the Netherlands by Willibrord, another Englishman. It equally inspired Bede who lived out his saintly and scholarly life in the monastery at Jarrow on the Tyne. Bede's own farewell is like an epitaph on the great flowering of monastic Christianity in the north of England at that time: "I have spent all my life in this monastery, applying myself entirely to the study of the Scriptures; and, amid the observance of the discipline of the Rule and the daily task of singing in the church, it has always been my delight to learn or to teach or to write....And I pray thee, merciful Jesus, that as thou hast graciously granted me sweet draughts from the Word which tells of Thee, so wilt thou, of thy goodness, grant that I may come at length to Thee, the fount of all wisdom and stand before thy face for ever." [4]

So brief a summary as this cannot do justice to the Benedictine achievement between Gregory the Great and the eleventh century. It was the time that inspired Newman to write:"Benedict found the world, physical and social, in ruins, and his mission was to restore it in the way, not of science, but of nature, not as if setting about to do it, not professing to do it by any set time or by any rare specific, or by any series of strokes, but so quietly, patiently, gradually, that often, till the work was done, it was not known to be doing.....The new world which he helped to create was a growth rather than a structure. Silent men were observed about the country, or discovered in the forest, digging, clearing and building; and other silent men, not seen, were sitting in the cold cloister, tiring their eyes, and keeping their attention on the stretch, while they painfully deciphered and copied and recopied the manuscripts which they had saved. There was no one that "contended, or cried out" or drew attention to what was going on; but by degrees the woody swamp became a hermitage, a religious house, a farm, an abbey, a village, a seminary, a school of learning, a city" 5

Newman's prose may not appeal to modern taste, but it does draw attention to the fact that the foundations for the new Europe of the Middle Ages and after were laid by monks and that the contribution of their lives was indispensible to the survival of that learning. The English Benedictines played a large part in that vast work, not only in England, but on the continent also.

Dunstan, Ethelwold and Oswald

AFTER THE DEVASTATION from overseas there was not much left of the Britain which had produced Bede, the Lindisfarne gospels, St Boniface and the Bodleian Rule of St Benedict. Alfred did something to encourage monastic communities but the real revival was in the following century. Dunstan became a monk at Glastonbury and in about 940 was made Abbot. He reformed the monastery by imposing the full observance of St Benedict's Rule. Then Edgar was made King of Wessex and he made Dunstan Archbishop of Canterbury. With Ethelwold he issued the Regularis Concordia – a code of directions for monastic observance which set the standard for monastic renewal throughout the country. With King Edgar he went on to a reform of Church and State. It was the second great flowering of monasticism. It was one in which Church and State were united as never before and never since.

Learning and the arts had suffered from the destruction or decline of the monastic centres of culture from which they had drawn their inspiration. By the middle of the century everything had changed. The Regularis Concordia had led to a revival of monastic ideals and of the zeal and creativeness that go with it. Three monks had been placed by the young king Edgar in key sees: Dunstan in Canterbury, Ethelwold in Winchester and Oswald in Worcester. Their influence was enormous. It stretched to every aspect of prayer, of learning, of the arts and of culture. It was an influence that gained much from the favour and encouragement of the King, but it went deeper than politics and power are capable of penetrating. There was something new about it and something that was intensely English. Like the Northumbrian Church of Cuthbert and Bede before the Norse invasions it was transparently faithful to the gospel and to the monastic ideal; but there was a difference. The strong and complex celtic influence of that northern flowering which produced the beautiful but abstract, remote and disturbing illuminations of the Lindisfarne Gospel gave way to something equally beautiful but more homely. The Anglo-Saxon line drawings of the manuscripts of Dunstan's day were intensely human. They reflected a direct and uncomplicated spirituality that is immediately understandable and appealing. Herbert Read suggests somewhere that, as line drawing, these monks' work was unsurpassed, and it has never been recaptured. It speaks of English Christianity at its purest and best, symbolising a new harmony between culture and spirituality. The monasticism, the learning and the culture of the time were at one. It was a precious time of integration.

"Under Edgar and Dunstan," writes Dom David Knowles,[6] "the revived monasticism had been the very heart and soul of the rebirth of the country; from the monasteries came the rulers of the Church for two generations, and the same men were the controlling influence in the social and political life of their times. In the monasteries, from 950 – 1050, was all that was purest in the spiritual, intellectual and artistic life of England. They were, indeed, especially between 950 and 1000, the very core and kernel of the nation and by their achievement in the transmission of the heritage of the past and in the execution of works of literature and art they have placed all succeeding generations in their debt. This phase of their life had passed before the Conquest, largely because its own inner force was spent. It never exactly repeated itself, for the nations of Europe had begun another chapter in their history."

Feudal Monasticism

THE CONQUEST by the Normans led to a new phase which was reflected in many aspects of monastic life and building. Nevertheless there was some continuity of the monastic ideal which had flowered so impressively in Anglo-Saxon times. Evesham Abbey, for instance, was sensitive to the old tradition. It was monks from Evesham who went north to re-found Wearmouth, Jarrow and Whitby. There were some Normans fully involved in this revival and the search for God was fully alive again in the north both through solitary and community life. In monasticism at least there was a convergence between Norman and Saxon traditions in the north.

Nevertheless, there were many changes after the conquest. When you look at the great monastic cathedrals which remain from the later mediaeval centuries and even at the Cistercian monastic ruins like Rievaulx and Fountains, it may seem that they are evidence of the high point of English monasticism, but they do not really represent the high point; what Dom David Knowles says is true. The Anglo-Saxon period was unique in its strength and purity. The influence of Feudalism on monasticism was in many respects regrettable and damaging. Both religious and secular life became more diffuse and varied with the rise of the Cathedral schools, and the Universities, and the coming of the Friars and other Orders. Life was more complex in every way. The monasteries became large and strong; perhaps they became too large and too strong and too powerful. The Abbots became great Lords with wide influence and their appointment a matter of secular concern and lamentable interference. The Abbot had a separate household and separate revenues.

Contrast that with a simple instruction which Gregory had sent to Augustine in one of his letters about how to go about converting the English: "Because you, brother, are conversant with monastic rules, and ought not to live apart from your clergy in the English Church, which, by the guidance of God, has lately been converted to the faith, you ought to institute that manner of life which our fathers followed in the earliest beginnings of the Church: none of them said that anything he possessed was his own, but they had all things in common." [7]

Whatever the eminence and importance of an Abbey the cross-currents of mediaeval life (both secular and ecclesiastical) often frustrated true monastic spirituality. How wrong things could go is illustrated by a particularly dramatic and disturbing example at Evesham Abbey in King John's reign: The Abbot died in 1189 and Archbishop Baldwin of Canterbury imposed one of his creatures, Roger Norreys, on the monks as their Abbot, against the monks' will, without a canonical election and in spite of the fact that he was notoriously unsuitable. As Abbot he lived a scandalous life, and neglected the administration and the needs of the community. Roger was skillful in playing off the King, the Bishop and the Pope against each other and the whole question was complicated by cross-issues of feudal and ecclesiastical rights. Matters were frozen during the interdict of 1207 to 1213 and only after that did the Papal legate successfully intervene and depose Roger Norreys. For twenty-five years a great Abbey had been in the grip of maladministration and scandal through no fault of the monks but because of a 'political' intervention – in this case of the Archbishop of Canterbury. And yet the true inner spirit of monasticism was not wholly lost. The Evesham Chronicle refers to a monk of that time named John Denis who for thirty years during all those troubles had lived in the monastery a life of exceptional prayer and penance, giving all that he could secure for them to the poor. [8]

The effects on monastic development which arose from the nature of the Feudal world of the middle ages is to be seen in quite a different way in the Cistercians, who are often called the White Benedictines because they wore a white habit. Their monasteries were founded deep in the country which gave them greater survival potential to fulfil the role of picturesque ruins which Jane Austen thought such an advantage to the English landscape. It was the Cistercians who built Rievaulx, Fountains, Byland, Furness, Melrose, Tintern. Their reform of the Benedictine way of life (for such it was) appeared on the monastic scene at the very beginning of the twelfth century at Citeaux in France on the borders of Brittany and Maine. It was an Englishman, Stephen Harding, who was the principle driving force among the founders (there were no national frontiers in the monastic world of the time). The Cistercian monastic vision was founded on an interpretation of the Rule of St Benedict which relied on a boundless, self-sacrificing zeal and a strictness which might well have caused a degree of surprise and concern to St Benedict himself. Manual work was elevated to a new central importance and many 'lay brothers' were recruited to work the land. Stephen Harding and his companions persevered in their very small beginnings in utter poverty for thirteen years until St Bernard joined them with thirty companions in 1112. His arrival signalled a creative explosion. In 1115 he founded Clairvaux. From then on the growth was astonishing. In England Waverley was founded in 1128,

Tintern in 1131, Rievaulx and Fountains in 1132. In a few years the Cistercians became an important part of the English monastic scene and remained so. They began, as they had at Citeaux, by taking over and cultivating in poverty wild and derelict land. But wild land which is cultivated becomes valuable, their donors were generous in the gift of many acres and the Cistercian development co-incided with a boom in sheep farming for the provision of wool. As their ruins show they became rich, so that to some extent the economics of the time tarnished their original vision of severe simplicity and poverty. The Cistercian Abbots became great Lords involved in the social fabric and their extensive agricultural properties important factors in the economic structure of the Country. Like the black-habited Benedictines they suffered from the effects of Feudalism. Their very success enmeshed them in dangers not at all of their own creating.

Nevertheless, in spite of the problems forced upon them, it must be remembered that the strong spirituality of St Benedict's Rule continued to bear hidden fruit in the lives of the monks both Benedictine and Cistercian. The assessments of historians, whether they are harsh in their criticism or sympathetic and idealistic, usually fail to touch the reality of individual lives which combine to make communities and institutions but which are never absorbed by them. When we reflect on the external history of a Benedictine Abbey this must be remembered. There were monks at all times who in St Benedict's phrase 'truly sought God' in the continuing framework of monastic life, whatever the problems brought by the times.

To get a full picture of Benedictine monasticism in England, mention should be made of the Alien Priories. From the coming of the Normans dependent priories were founded in England by Benedictine houses on the continent. The most notable of these foreign founding houses was the great French Abbey of Cluny which had as many as 38 English dependencies, most of which were small. The outbreak of the hundred years war made them the target of criticism and in 1414 Parliament sought the sequestration of their lands and property. It was the first political move against Benedictine houses but it may be too fanciful to see it, as some historians do, as the model for Henry VIII's work a century later. It was the first move towards confiscation, but the motive was nationalist not religious. The concern was not that they were Benedictine Priories but that they were alien.

Problems, then, for the Benedictine houses had undoubtedly increased during the fifteenth and early sixteenth centuries, but they were due to lack of numbers and the laxness of the times rather than to rank infidelity. The fire of earlier days had gone. But the spirit of St Benedict is so strong that it can survive even in bad times, and the inner spirit of an Abbey and the individual monks in it is not always revealed by its external status. Nevertheless the decline of the English Benedictine Black Monks – and of the Cistercian White Monks also – was unmistakable in the later Middle Ages particularly after the black death. It is arguable that there were too many religious houses of all kinds and by the fifteenth century there were not enough monks in the communities to justify the great buildings they inherited. It was clear to those with their best interests at heart that the Benedictines were in need of reform and renewal. It was and is less obvious that the best way of reforming the monks was to abolish them, but that was the conclusion imposed with ruthless violence by Henry VIII.

In the four years between 1536 and 1540 one hundred and thirty seven houses of English Benedictine Black monks were closed. The monastic cathedrals and Westminster Abbey survived into the new dispensation. In addition thirty-one houses of monks from foreign Benedictine Congregations were closed and 85 Cistercian houses. Thus 253 centres of that monastic spirituality which had come with Augustine ceased to exist. The cathedrals escaped destruction but were purged of monasticism and one or two monastic houses, like Chester, were reprieved so that they might provide cathedral churches for new Anglican dioceses.

Survival and Renewal

BY THE END of the sixteenth century England had moved into a new age, into new perspectives, new knowledge, new visions and the New World. For those in political power at the time the new world was to be purged of any trace of monasticism. Was it right from now on for the English people to be deprived of anything to recall the monasticism which had been so integral to English Christian life except a few romantic ruins and the cathedral churches stripped of everything that might recall the monastic past which had created them? As time went on that certainly seemed to be the perspective of those who had the power to decide and to impose their decision. A minority thought differently and went abroad to found new English Benedictine monasteries to preserve the ancient and strong monastic tradition of the church in England.

The Benedictines in mediæval England held a unique position in the Church and society. They were responsible for seven of the Cathedrals including Canterbury. The Cathedral Prior held the position of an Anglican dean and the community that of the Chapter. There were fifty Abbots and Cathedral Priors in the House of Lords. Henry VIII put an end to all that. Nothing was left when it came to the settlement under Elizabeth. However in the first decade of the seventeenth century when some young Englishmen crossed the Channel to become Benedictines they forged a link with the mediæval Benedictines through one surviving monk from the community of Westminster Abbey which had been restored by Queen Mary and then dissolved again by

Elizabeth. That link had a juridical as well as an emotional validity. The old Congregation of Benedictines was revived and refounded in the new English Benedictine Congregation which took shape at first on the Continent and then at the outbreak of the French Revolution in England again. That continuity of the Congregation is unique; there was no parallel continuity in the other European Benedictine houses in the face of the onslaught of the Reformation, the French Revolution and Napoleon. The English Benedictine link with Westminster means that, since St Augustine's arrival fourteen hundred years ago, there has been a Benedictine continuity right up to the present day. The English Benedictine spirit did not die completely.

It was in 1607 that the last of the old Benedictines of Westminster Abbey witnessed the profession of two young monks and then affiliated them to the Marian foundation of Westminster. The motive was conscious and deliberate; it was to preserve intact the living Benedictine commitment which had meant so much in the Christian life of this country since Augustine of Canterbury. Through that affiliation the link was passed on to the two Houses that formed the nucleus of the renewed Congregation: St Gregory's which was established at Douai and St Laurence's which began life at Dieulouard. Both communities prospered as Benedictine priories for Englishmen in France and were strongly conscious of their continuity with the mediæval English Benedictines. The apostolic dimension, which had begun with the first mission of St Augustine, was revived also and confirmed in papal documents. The monks supported the English Catholics during the years of persecution by sending priests to serve them. Some of these monks gave their lives as martyrs for their faith. This apostolic work continued after the return to England in parishes which were later incorporated into the Abbeys. Everything changed, however, when the French Revolution came. In spite of the loss of all their property the two communities escaped to England. Eventually St Laurence's settled at Ampleforth in 1802 and St Gregory's at Downside in 1814. When peace came a third English house, St Edmund's, which had been established in Paris, was refounded in the Benedictine buildings in Douai from which St Gregory's had been driven at the time of the revolution. St Edmund's remained and prospered as an English House in France until the French laws against religious houses of 1903, when they moved to Woolhampton in Berkshire. There they retained the name of Douai. In the revival of the early seventeenth century two Benedictine communities of English nuns had been founded at Cambrai in 1625 and at Paris in 1651. They also escaped from France and settled respectively at Stanbrook near Worcester and at Colwich in Staffordshire. These together with the three Houses of monks, St Gregory's Downside, St Laurence's Ampleforth and St Edmund's Douai formed the nucleus which survived the Revolution and re-established the English Benedictine Congregation on English soil.

Since then other houses have joined the original five of the English Benedictine Congregation: Fort Augustus in Scotland, Belmont, Ealing, Buckfast, Worth, and in USA there are three founded from England, Washington, Portsmouth and St Louis. There is also a third EBC convent for nuns at Curzon Park in Chester. To complete the picture of restoration it should be added that besides the above mentioned houses of the English Benedictine Congregation other

Benedictine houses for the English have been founded by other Congregations, namely Quarr Abbey from the Solesmes Congregation, Ramsgate, Prinknash, Pluscarden and Farnborough from the Subiaco Congregation, Cockfosters and Turvey from the Olivetan Congregation; and there are convents for nuns following the Rule of St Benedict like Tyburn in London and Fernham in Oxfordshire, Minster in Kent, Oulton in Staffordshire, and others who take much of their inspiration from St Benedict's Rule, like the Sisters of Grace and Compassion.

The White Benedictines or Cistercians, who were so numerous in England in the Middle Ages and are remembered by the ruins of such Abbeys as Rievaulx, Fountains and Tintern, returned to England in the nineteenth century in the foundation of Mount Saint Bernard's Abbey near Leicester. They were joined by Caldey Abbey, on an island off the coast near Tenby, and Nunraw Abbey in Scotland. In addition, there is a convent of Cistercian nuns at Holy Cross Abbey in South Wales.

The Benedictines, then, are back. It is not extravagant to suggest that they are at home again and that they never left the country they helped so much to mould in its first response to Christianity. There is a sense of local attachment and moderate independence which is integral to the Benedictine spirit, because it is enshrined in the Rule of St Benedict. The English took kindly to it once, and some have wondered whether that same spirit, so familiar in the England of Saxon times and the Middle Ages, has actually survived in the hearts of English men and women, although they were left for three centuries with little but ruins to remind them of it? Is there some degree of affinity between Benedictine spirituality and at least some elements of Anglicanism? Some see it in the psalmody of the Prayer Book and the tradition of antiphonal singing. Then there are the Cathedrals with the Abbey churches which were retained by the Anglican establishment. They remained, and they remained in sacred use. Those that had been Benedictine preserved the memory at least as vividly as the romantic ruins and with more promise of life. The country is still dotted with them: Canterbury, Norwich, Ely, Peterborough, Durham, Chester, Worcester, Tewkesbury, Winchester, Westminster. They were built for the Benedictine round of liturgical prayer every day and every night. There are some who sense the echo of that prayer still when they visit and pray in the buildings built by the monks for God.

"Like so many Anglicans", writes Esther de Waal, "I had been aware of this country's monastic heritage in buildings and works of art.....I was simply one of the many who admired abbey ruins and cathedral cloisters for what they said about past greatness. But actually to come and live in Canterbury in the context of that greatness was an entirely different experience......One day an excavation...in the area of the monastic graveyard came upon two skeletons. As they lay there, anonymous, individual and yet corporate, I found myself suddenly confronted with the men whose hands had built this place and whose vision had created its way of life. That encounter led me to read the Rule of St Benedict. I felt that I needed to discover something of the spirit of Benedictine life......Sometimes one finds a place, a landscape, which is new and yet the forms, the shapes, the shadows seem already familiar. So it was for me with the Rule. It was neither remote, nor past nor cerebral, but immediate and relevant, speaking of things that I already half knew or was struggling to make sense of. It tackled with honesty questions of personal relationships and authority and freedom; it recognised the need for stability and the need for change; it established a pattern for a balanced life; its sense of respect and reverence for people and for material things touched me immediately. I valued its insight on such day-to-day matters as hospitality or the attitude towards material possessions. Above all it spoke of a life that was essentially unheroic, much in fact like the life of any ordinary Christian family." [9]

Esther de Waal's words are not a romantic fantasy. They reflect the truth that the spirit of St Benedict is essentially founded in Scripture and the Fathers of the Church. The same sources have been strong in the traditions of Anglicanism, particularly since the Oxford Movement. It is small wonder that in the twentieth century there has been a new development of Benedictine life within the Anglican Communion in Elmore and Alton Abbey for men and in West Malling, Edgware, Burford, Holy Cross Rempstone and St Hilda's Whitby for women. These Anglican Benedictines come together with Catholic monks and nuns in the Union of Monastic Superiors, where a shared monastic vision strengthens and deepens the growth of ecumenical understanding.

The secret of Benedictine revival and renewal is that the spirit of St Benedict is timeless and it still fits the modern scene surprisingly well. It is timeless because it is modelled so closely on the word of Scripture; it fits because it offers the inspiration and vision so sadly lacking in the spiritual desert of today.

Spiritual Vision for Yesterday and Today

WHEN GREGORY SENT Augustine to Kent to preach the gospel, it was an odd thing to do, especially for a Benedictine Pope. Benedictines weren't meant to be sent across the world on apostolic missions. Benedictines are not a centralised Order with a specific work or range of works. The idea of such a centralised order did not exist and it was not invented until the Friars came in the thirteenth century. Each Benedictine Abbey is a separate and independent community. Nowadays, although they are still independent and separate so that a monk or nun belongs to one community always, Benedictine Abbeys are linked by federation to form Congregations. The idea of such a federation of independent communities of monks was first thought of at the Lateran Council of 1215. The English Benedictines followed that lead and formed a loose affiliation of Houses – the English Benedictine Congregation. But the idea didn't take root on the continent. It was not until the nineteenth century revival of Benedictine life that the Congregations became a general reality. It was only a hundred years ago that a wider affiliation was set up between the various Benedictine Congregations to form the Benedictine Confederation, but this is not a centralised power structure in a way comparable to the organisation of the friars or the post-Reformation apostolic orders of men and women. Benedictine affiliation is real, but it is not for control and unification but for support and encouragement and mutual help. The individual Abbeys are still independent local communities under the rule of their own Abbot, as St Benedict intended.

The work Benedictines do has historically arisen from the need to earn their living, from the needs of the local church and from what they had to offer through just living their community life. The idea of giving them missionary work was Pope Gregory's, but on his instructions they carried it out in a peculiarly Benedictine way without any infringement of the central genius of the Rule. You remember how they acted under his guidance: they preached by prayer; they attracted by example; they helped and sustained through their own stability and commitment. St Benedict had urged the Abbot to rule rather by example than by precept. That was exactly the spirit of St Gregory's advice to St Augustine about how to convert the English.

So it happened that the sort of work that suited Benedictines well was local pastoral work, the sharing of their daily liturgy and hospitality and sharing with the local laity the gifts they had themselves. St Benedict says, as though appealing to the obvious, that a monastery is never without guests and that they must all be received as Christ himself. In today's world retreats, spiritual counselling and renewal and catechesis both of the young and adults fit very well into Benedictine life. Then there is Benedictine education which began from the first with the education of young monks in the monastery. It soon happened that, because the expertise for learning and teaching was there as part of the Benedictine way of living, lay students were taken in and small monastic schools became common. In the nineteenth and twentieth centuries some Benedictine schools in Europe and America have grown large and famous. Many Benedictine houses are able to continue this great work today at secondary and tertiary level.

Benedictines have often owned large farms and cared for them well, so that they became leaders in the development of agriculture; but the actual work was not normally done by the monks as part of their daily routine, except among the white Benedictines or Cistercians. A certain amount of manual labour was normal but it was not the main occupation of the black monks or Benedictines. This was not their purpose any more than their other daily works were.

If in the past or today you asked what Benedictines are for – if you demanded what is now fashionable, namely A Mission Statement, then in a practical way one could talk of any of the above works in the sense that each is typical of what Benedictines do; but one would have to add that none of them could possibly form the purpose of Benedictine life. The purpose of the Benedictine vocation is to seek God in commitment to community prayer and community living. In all they do the Work of God (as St Benedict describes their prayer) comes first at all times. The Work of God is the daily round of community prayer which they offer in the Abbey Church. That is what Benedictines exist for – to offer worship to God and pray for the salvation of mankind. Everything else that they do flows from that prayer.

Incidentally for a community to devote itself to such worship of God and prayer for the church and mankind is itself an effective witness to faith; it is also an effective weapon of evangelisation – the one with which St Augustine converted the wild men of Kent and St Boniface the peoples of Germany. Such God-centred witness in a strong spiritual centre is something much needed today. It is needed as never before in our contemporary world, where Christian faith and the life it inspires are at such a discount. "Practice unsupported by belief is a wasting asset" said Toynbee. By contrast belief manifested in practice is a spiritual asset of incomparable power.

However you express it, however you look at it, the Benedictine vision, which was in the past so much part of the development of Christianity in this country, is centred not on doing, but on being, not on programmes about achieving, but on a way of living which radiates gospel values and welcomes others to them in the context of disciplined community prayer and total commitment to God.

At the end of his Rule St Benedict put down his pen with the work complete. Then, he thought further (as one does after writing anything, however good). He thought further and then he took up his pen again to add something, and this is what he wrote:

> "Just as there is a wicked zeal of bitterness which separates from God and leads to self-destruction, so there is a good zeal which separates from evil and leads to God and everlasting life. This, then, is the good zeal which monks must foster with fervent love. They should each be the first to show respect to the other, supporting with the greatest patience one another's weaknesses whether of body or behaviour and competing to obey each other's needs. No-one is to pursue what he judges better for himself, but instead what he judges better for another. To their fellow monks let them show the pure love of brothers, to God loving fear, to their Abbot unfeigned and un-demanding love. And let them prefer nothing

whatever to Christ; and may he bring us all together to everlasting life." [10]

St Benedict is concerned in this chapter not with rules and regulations, not with the external circumstances of life, not with riches or poverty, not with different cultures, different customs, different traditions, different languages. He ends his spiritual message with no precepts, no prohibitions, no attempts to regulate the externals of life. He ends with a powerful expression of the inner spirit he is concerned to pass on. Without that spirit, he implies, externals can achieve nothing; with it any external circumstances will be transformed and, however threatening they may be, they cannot overcome.

Many years ago I attended an educational conference. Fortunately it was not confined in its clientele to educationalists. There were interesting outside delegates from industry and commerce. I sat one morning over coffee with a Polish ex-patriate, who was a successful engineer. He told me that he was seventeen when the Communists invaded his country from Russia. He was transported from a happy home to one of those 'camps'. I offered him my sympathy over the experience and speculated on how terrible it must have been. I found no response of self-pity; he did not warm to the prospect of making a display of his remembered misery; he had no interest in satisfying my curiosity about the horrors that had been familiar to him and had never touched my protected life. He said that none of those things mattered. What mattered was this, he said: he was now exactly the same person he had been in the camps with exactly the same spiritual problems to face. For instance, he said, when he was in the camp he would be absorbed for days, for weeks, with his plans and efforts to get hold of a tin can which had contained processed food. If he got this and succeeded in keeping it to drink from, he would be like a king. In those days he had nothing and the tin meant everything to him. Now, he had a good job, a loving family, but he was still the same inside. It wasn't a tin now, but he was planning, dreaming, longing to own a beautiful and expensive boat in which he could take his son sailing. "You see," he said, "The spirit within is the same. I have not grown spiritually. My life is dependent on things." My comment was that he had grown more than he would admit. His honesty and the clarity of his self-perception was an inestimable gift. I have forgotten absolutely everything else about that conference, but I can never forget my Polish friend and brother, whom I met over coffee and who taught me so much.

It is that inner spirit, which my Polish prophet could so clearly and unusually distinguish from external circumstances (however savage they were), that concerns St Benedict in Chapter 72. It is the only ground on which our lives can be ultimately judged. It is so with Benedictine monasteries. The size of a monastery, the external works, the wealth it can dispose of or the poverty with which it must struggle at any given time are secondary to the spirit within.

Through so many centuries Benedictine monasteries have contributed in varying degrees to Christian life in Britain. Sometimes the heart of their vocation has been obscured – sometimes it has been manifest; but they have never been so effective in their prayer and work nor so faithful to the original monastic mission of St Augustine as when they have been really faithful to the spirit of that chapter 72 which St Benedict added to his original draft of the Rule.

Notes

1. *A Toynbee* Civilisation on Trial n 12.

2. *W Shakespeare* Hamlet Act V Scene III.

3. *Bede* History of the English Church & People 1, 26.

4. *Bede* History of the English Church & People 5, 224.

5. *JH Newman* The Mission of the Benedictine Order.

6. *D Knowles* The Monastic Order in England p.680.

7. *Bede* History of the English Church & People 1, 27.

8. *D Knowles* The Monastic Order in England ch. XIX.

9. *E de Waal* Seeking God. The Benedictine Way.

10. The Rule of St Benedict ch. 72.

FURTHER READING

Abbot Justin McCann OSB *Saint Benedict*

Dom David Knowles OSB *The Monastic Order in England*

Dom Timothy Fry OSB *RB80: The Rule of Saint Benedict*

Abbot Georg Holzherr OSB *The Rule of Benedict: A Guide to Christian Living*

Adalbert de Vogué OSB *The Rule of Saint Benedict: A Doctrinal and Spiritual Commentary*

Abbot David Parry OSB & Esther de Waal *The Rule of Saint Benedict with Commentary*

David Hugh Farmer *Benedict's Disciples*

Dom Wulstan Mork OSB *The Benedictine Way*

Esther de Waal *Seeking God: The Benedictine Way*

Esther de Waal *Living with Contradiction: Reflections on the Rule of Saint Benedict*

Esther de Waal *A Life-giving Way: A Commentary on the Rule of Saint Benedict*

Abbot Columba Cary-Elwes OSB *Work and Prayer: The Rule of Saint Benedict for Lay People*

Brian C Taylor *Spirituality for Everyday Living: An Adaptation of the Rule of Saint Benedict*